the
YOGINI

Shree Krishna & Dr. Neharika saxena

BlueRose ONE
Stories Matter
NewDelhi • London

BlueRose ONE
Stories Matter
NewDelhi • London

For permissions requests or inquiries regarding this publication,
please contact:

BLUEROSE PUBLISHERS
www.BlueRoseONE.com
info@bluerosepublishers.com
+91 8882 898 898
+4407342408967

ISBN: 978-93-6452-046-1

Cover design: Shivam
Typesetting: Namrata Saini

First Edition: July 2024

Acknowledgement

I would like to thank Lord Krishna, the supreme king, for being the sole author of this book who plays the role of all divine beings by his Maya. This book is a gift of love to Lord Krishna. I seek your blessings and devotion in every life I get. My regards to this beautiful universe and our amazing galaxy Milky way. To dear Sun god and to all our nine planets of our solar system.

To my parents Dr. Hari Mohan saxena whose love is incomparable to the best riches of the world and (Late mother) Dr Madhu prabha saxena for all her sacrifice and help in bringing me up in life. To my grandmother Mrs Kamla saxena for taking care of me like a mother (P.S. I love you) and to my younger sister Priyanka saxena for bieng an amazing sister.

To sisters Radharani and Rukminiji for their compassion and help in Krishna consciousness. My love to sister Subhadraji and Brother Dauji.

Table of Contents

The Yogini

It was misty dusk
the cloudy dawn
There appeared the lamb and the fawn
Out of the sky he appeared
The one who's loved by everyone
He lifted my veil with an admiring gaze
As if all the strife disappeared
His eyes beamed with a beautiful gleam
It felt like a lore or a dream
My Lord was there
And it was him
so lost was I in his bountiful joy
The sky was clear and it softly rained
In the myriad of his curls,
So lost was I, yet I took a stance
My drop dead gorgeous
So intertwined like in a trance
Two hearts but One soul
I forgot my chalice and my wine
unto your sweet melody divine
To the sound of your flute
Still echoes in my heart
Does your heart still beat for me?

I asked as I looked into his eyes

He smiled and then nodded yes

Make a passion and he said that resonates with the sound of my beating heart

With kisses that are so sublime

With poetry sub missed in your verse

Where can I take you my handsome lord, I smiled

Where to hide thy benevolent smile

He smiled softly paused and said

I am an ocean, and you a lake

Meet me where the swans meet

And where the moon shines

At the zenith of your heart's desire

He kissed her forehead and then caressed her hair

To meet me real, you have travelled long

Stop now your wait

I waited and waited long I said

Long's been the journey and the days gone by

Come to me my lover in a quick embrace

Don't think of the monsters

And Be brave

and I'll take you to stars

To the moon in space

And Lo he kissed me so

That all my pain and fears gone

Lo beloved he embraced me so

That all the fiery monsters disappeared
And then our feisty journey began
From the abyss of dismay
To the fields of lovers glory
So this is the beginning of my story..

This is the true story of a young girl named Misha..who crossed the seas and dimensions to reach her true love.

Chapter 1

The Fortune Teller

Misha was a doctor by profession..but she believed in magic.

Misha was lonely but she always believed in the concept of soulmate and wanted one for herself. So she approached a fortune teller to gain insight into her future.

In a White bungalow between the houses somewhere in Jaipur, lived a fortune teller named Maya. She was famous for her esoteric insight and tarot readings.

Misha decided to consult her. She went to her place with a friend. It was afternoon so there were not so many people at the reception. Soon her turn came. She felt uneasy as she sat in front of Maya. She had a strange mystic aura on her face with wavy hairs that fell in curls below.

"Now tell, What is it that you want to ask?" Asked the psychic I want to know if I will ever get my soulmate or not? asked Misha anxiously

She prayed to god as the fortune teller spread out the tarot cards and asked her to choose a few. She obeyed.The mysterious fortune teller looked at her face, smiled and said as she picked a card of Ace.

"An unusual lover but divine, true in his form and supreme in might..You shall meet him in a tryst,in this small village of Ithaca,Cornell."

Maya, the fortune teller, told her that soulmate would be somewhere in this beautiful village of Ithaca in Cornell,USA.

She didn't understand at first,as she hadn't heard the name of Ithaca before. "Where is it located" asked Misha. Maya asked the holy spirits with tarot cards "It's somewhere in New York,in the states" answered she. Okay.. Misha noted down.Then her friend Nitika also asked her questions from the tarot. Maya smiled and satisfied them with her answers.The girls were happy as they went back home after paying Maya's fee.

Misha went to a cybercafe to search for the place as android mobiles were not available in those days.

It was a beautiful place as she scrolled down the net for its photos.

It was one of those weird Deja vu's that she felt. Maybe the fortune teller was right. But She was a simpleton from a small town of Ludhiana who could only dream of an Ivy league college like Cornell in a place like Ithaca.

Then came the superhit concept of "The Secret" by Rhonda Byran.

She worked hard on her grade point in degree and made a nice CV by her accomplishment and determination.

She breathed Cornell, She dreamt Cornell. Even visualized herself there. It had become her life's mission now.

After four years of penance by using the secret law of attraction, It works and you'll be surprised to know that she attracted an opportunity to visit Cornell in which She was selected to represent India abroad in a student exchange program. Her parents were on cloud nine.

Tickets were booked, Passports and visa..made ready.

The day of journey came.

Her eyes gleamed with hope of success as she boarded the plane that would change her destiny. She dreamt of becoming an astronaut one day and maybe finding her soulmate as well. She looked below at the beaming sky flowered with clouds everywhere. Crossing the grasslands and the seas..she was a warrior in her eyes today.

Sitting in the plane she wrote a poem for her soulmate, who she believed will meet her in Cornell. Sometimes its great to be young and dreamy..

She wrote as her plane crossed over the sea,the lights of plane flashed on the window..as she wrote

In love forever after ..

I crossed the seven seas for you
Strolled in the woods and upon hill tops
Many a meadows I crossed in vain
Lonely with sighs I wept in rain,
Of many a hearts covess was I
Sometimes with pain,sometimes with pride
Love lorn I wandered like a litter lout
But my heart coveted for a clout
When love became a never ending pursuit,
Lost myself with the winds aloof..
Some thought me a maniac, and some a fool
I travelled wide a million miles
And one day in this little strife
Our eyes met in a little tryst
And then he smiled with a little blush
For it was not him but his soul that blushed
And aloha!he said with a smile
And again we meet today
For so long in my dreams
In my heart you dwelled
For my love my princess
I love you so
For I was searching for you as well
And gusto!he embraced me so

Alludes in my beats

You have been my soul

The stars I have followed in you're pursuit

And darling you look great in a suit!

Come closer to me, and let my pain disappear

It rained that day,and he came near

He touched my soul and I had no fear

For he was my love,my mate, my peer

All that you crossed was not in vain

For it takes some pain, some bane for a gain

True love I found in life's mayhem

With me as you're love and you as my helm

I fell for you're heart and not you're hesiodic charm

And every day you're smile just makes it so warm

To this I touched his lips and said

Shh.. be quiet all done and said

Doth know ye not

How long my strife

Who knows what next moment brings to life

And before the busy fret of life begins

Let me dream and let me dance,

Just be with you and in you're trance

She crunched up some chips and folded the paper on which poem was written, to gift it to her soulmate which she believed that she'll meet in Cornell. Faith is a very powerful thing. Lets see what destiny has in store for her..The waitress came and gave her some coke.She was a chips freak and loved it. The night came and she dozed off after watching the movie Shrek on TV screen tucked in the back of front seat. One can't imagine the joy that was bubbling inside her. Such a quantum leap of faith was hard to take and yet it became possible due to the Secret. Thankyou Rhonda Byran.

Soon America arrived and they landed in Ithaca. There were many people at the gate waiting for their acquaintances. She saw some decent old gentlemen holding a placard with "Welcome Misha" on it. She ran towards them. Are you Misha? One of them asked curiously. Yes and you must be Dr. David and Dr….? asked Misha.

"Dr. Robin is my name, Welcome to America" the other gentleman greeted.

So they sat in Dr. Robin's car and drove to Cornell university. After arriving she checked in a sorority where other exchange students from different countries were already present with their bags and stuff. After some pleasantries with other fellows she went to sleep in her room.

It was a pretty room with a cute almirah and a double seater bed. The place was lush full of beauty and greenery, with flowers blooming like from a fairy tale. Everything seemed so perfect and divine.

Chapter 2

The Annoying Kacy

She spent a few days wandering Ithaca and checking out the restaurants.The masonry clock tower known as McGraw Tower is situated on the Cornell University campus. Mainly played by student chimes masters, the 21 bells are housed in the historic McGraw Tower. She adored the melodious Cornell clock tower bell. Every hour, songs were played. She loved the ice cream place where she loved being alone with her ice cream.

She was amazed by the combination of the frozen sweetness and the sprinkles. She could feel her veins filling with endorphins. It was like tasting summer differently with every mouthful.

It was fun to roam around with curious fellow mates of her, exploring wine night outs. But soon they were allotted projects to work on under their respective mentors in their labs.

They started working meticulously for their weekly report. Misha was laborious and learnt Gel Electrophoresis technique there.

But She had a jealous and annoying lab assistant there name Kacy. She was a part time lab attendant and a research fellow. One day they were discussing PCR protocol (A lab technique to amplify DNA) Misha was not able to understand some basic chemistry as she had forgotten the method of making a particular volume of solution.

"Do you understand english?" asked Kacy angrily. Misha meekly nodded.

Kacy said "I know you are from a lame Institute in India but this is Cornell and we need excellent researchers here". She then started scolding her in front of everyone. Misha had no option but to listen. She was not well versed in molecular techniques. It left her in tears. She cried for half an hour before starting her work again.

"Excuse me"..came a voice from behind "Can I borrow your normal saline solution..".

Misha wiped her tears and looked at him. He was a very handsome guy, brazillian in accent.

"Sure"..she smiled.. "here it is" as she handed him the solution. "I am Carlos from the adjoining Dr. Fords's lab. He said as he made her blush. He smiled to that.

"I am Misha" she said as she shyly shook his hand. They often met in lab where he would talk to her on pretext of asking chemicals. They soon became friends. Handsome as he was, she started having a crush on him.Maybe he is the one I am searching for.. She thought. One day one of her labmates gifted her a T shirt on which Cornell was printed in bold letters, Misha wore it. Hi.. greeted Carlos how are you?

I am fine said Misha hiding her blush. "So what is this T-shirt you are wearing?" he asked. "Oh this I got it from the library, they are distributing free T shirts there."

"Lets go to the library" said Misha, excited at the prospect of getting freebies.

So they went to the library to the counter where they were distributing T- shirts.

Misha grasped one T shirt,Carlos took two of them.

"I will take two" he said " as I need one for my wife"..

What! wife.. looked Misha at him "Carlos are you married?" She looked in disbelief.

"Yes dear my wife lives with me here"Said Carlos.

Oh.. I thought you were single..fluttered Misha

(Oh god this guy is married..so silly of me) Thought Misha

Carlos smiled at Misha as if he could read her thoughts and took her by hand "Come with me" he said

He introduced her to his wife who was waiting for him in another lab. Pretty as she was, her flawless personality made Misha wonder where she stood in front of her.

Carlos then took her to another lab "see her she will help you here" said Carlos pointing to a Pakistani girl.

Her name was Nazma and she could speak in urdu which is very similar to hindi spoken in India. She was a scientist in a reputed college in Pakistan and was in Cornell for a research project.

Misha was overjoyed to meet her. "Hii I am Nazma" said she. "I am Misha. Nice to meet you" smiled Misha with sad eyes still loitering with thoughts of Carlos's wife, but she was happy that she found someone who she could talk to in hindi for this foriegn culture was very different for her.

"So I'll take a leave ladies,I have some work, boss called" said Carlos as he left.

"So Nazma where in Pakistan are you from?" asked Misha

"I am from Lahore" she said smiling back "and you?"

"I am from Ludhiana,India" replied Misha

So they became friends. Misha discussed her research problems with Nazma and she readily agreed to help her. She would work at odd hours at night around 2-5 am with Misha bieng scared at the very thought of it. She taught her how to work with centrifuge and other lab machines. Nazma loved working like that. She purposely chose odd hours so that there would be no trouble with other lab mates.

One day Misha was waiting for Nazma at the lab at 3 am. Suddenly Nazma's message flashed on the phone "Sorry I won't be able to come tonight due to some emergency". Misha couldn't go out at night so she decided to wait in lab for day to arrive. She started strolling through Ithaca chat rooms where she had enrolled before. Someone had sent her a friend request.His name was Zeus. Pictures of a very handsome man flashed on the screen. Misha was overjoyed..Wow and He is a Brazillian. So they chatted late night they struck a chord with each other. This friendship continued for few days and Zeus asked Misha out on a date.

On the particular date they decided to meet under the Mc Graw clock Tower. That tower plays musical bells after every quarter. When Misha and Zeus arrived the song played "Taylor Swift,Love story". The song played "we were both young when I first saw you"...

The atmosphere became magical as soft droplets of rain added to the mist.

Hear this song and feel what Misha felt at that particular moment. Zeus and Misha then went to a candy cafe nearby where they sold candies.

Misha loved candies so it was like a perfect date for her. Zeus held her hand and kissed it. They then went to a nearby lake where they spent some quality time with each other. It was like a dream come true for her,and the romance got the better of her.

In a weeks time they became sweethearts, soon Zeus's birthday arrived and Misha got a gift for him,and a nice dress for the evening with a white rose hairclip. She looked like a bride in that dress. Zeus was overjoyed to see her at his home. He loved his gift and smelled her fragrance. It was too much for a man to bear. She then played a very romantic song for him and they danced softly. Then he kissed her and kissed her some more.They then sat at the bed and continued kissing each other.

Wow! The time has arrived. There is no point of saying no to this guy thought Misha so she decided to go with the flow. She softly kissed his ears and neck, they passionately made love to each other with every thrust with every touch they got closer and closer so much so that in his passionate embrace Misha lost her soul. It was beautiful. Zeus went to another room to get something .Suddenly she saw divine light shining on the wall. It was god. He was smiling at their passion. She got up to greet him and got up in regard covering herself with a blanket.

He blessed her and then dissappeared. Misha felt blessed..maybe it was god's wish that they make love with each other. At night Zeus's face became more beautiful with soft moonlight kissing his lips and fragrance of rose embracing his arms. In the morning Zeus made her coffee and said " It was lovely what happened last night. Our relationship has just started and it happened too soon" he said. It was clear that Zeus was in love.

"What relationship!" Misha exclaimed She freaked out at that moment. "You are bieng bitchy Misha" a voice said in her mind but she was not ready for commitment,maybe it was too soon and that too with a foreigner.

"Oh!" Zeus changed his expression he felt hurt and used,

but he jokingly said "you came with bad intentions".

Misha smiled "oh common."She realised that Zeus had sincere feelings for her.

One day Zeus called her up. They met at the basketball court on Sunday. Misha was overjoyed. They became passionate with each other. It was divine again.Every moment spent together was like an elixir from heaven.She decided to not be serious for him as it made her vulnerable. They would meet up in their spare time and Zeus had lots to share.

His sincerity changed her heart and she fell in love with him, but it was a bit late.

She had hurt his ego and a man's ego is a fragile thing. He was no longer interested in a relationship.

They didn't talk too much after that. She wanted to tell him but she wasn't able to.

She came sometimes to meet him but he was not very pleasant and ignored her.

Misha was heartbroken. She became ill with shizophrenia.

One day she saw him at the bus stop, chatting and giggling with another girl.

Possessive as she was she talked to Zeus a little bit and ran away crying thinking maybe this is his new girlfriend. Now she was sure that Zeus was not the man she was searching for.

In her loneliness she decided to talk to ghosts. She started talking to spirits on ouija boards to talk to god. The was a suicide bridge nearby. Many people had committed suicide there . The spirits started haunting her. The world of ghosts had opened for her. They would scare her day and night. Even beat her up at times. Misha was shit scared.

She decided to search for her soulmate with sincerity. She consulted a psychic. The psychic said you were Radha rani in last birth that's why your soulmate is lord Krishna. Misha was amazed at that. Although the psychic only intended to fool her to make money but Misha believed every word she said.

She started imagining herself to be Radharani. Misha's happiness had no bound. She would talk to psychics more often now. Spending lots of money on them. They would often fool her. One day at 2 am at night she heard melodious bansuri somewhere near the a pond near Ezra Cornell's house. She rushed there crossing the suicide bridge with great courage.She waited all night near the pond but no one came.

Tears welled up in her soft doe eyes. She called the psychic next day.

The only thing she wanted was to hear a message from her beloved.

"How is Lord Krishna?" asked Misha

"I can see him smiling" said the psychic "He says he loves you a lot."

"I want to meet him. Please ask him where should I meet him" curiosity got the better of her, getting anxious to see her lover for whom she had crossed seven seas.

"He will meet you at the bus stop"said she "Now that is 100$ please.. your time is over".

"No.. I will give you more money" fluttered Misha. The psychic was the only way for her to contact her beloved Krishna, but the daily limit of her account was over that's why the bank had sealed her credits for the day.

In the evening, she went to the bus stop and waited for 2 hours there, but no one came.

She called the psychic once again and the psychic fooled her again.

To make matters worse shizophrenia got the better of her. She would talk to psychics to talk to Krishna and they would fool her laundering her money. Every sitting costed her 50$. She became broke but it cudn't break her spirit. She would wait at the pond in the night waiting for her beloved to arrive.

In the day she would do her research work somehow and in the evening she would ponder at Lord Krishna's handsomeness. At night there was a long wait near the pond. She would sometimes hear bansuri playing nearby which would make her happy.

Nazma (her pakistani friend) meanwhile had finished her project. She had to go back to her country Pakistan but she no longer had any place to stay as her lease contract had finished so she moved in with Misha.

"You are so kind Misha" Nazma would say "that you let me stay in your room."

"I see my benefit in that" replied Misha. She said so as it protected her from the ghosts that haunted her. They would still harass her but Nazma helped Misha to get over them, now Misha was no longer afraid as Nazma was with her. Nazma would read the holy Kuran for her so that the ghosts couldn't harass her. When her time to go came Nazma bid her farewell as Nazma's uncle had come to pick her up who lived in another state in USA.

One day there was a party at her sodority. Her friend introduced her to a very handsome man. He was ethereally handsome. Curly brown hairs, deep brown eyes.Greek god like features. A smile that would make any maiden go gaga. To her surprise he came and sat next to her.

"Hi!" Said he "you are Misha right"

"Yes" said Misha surprised "How do you know?"

(Such a handsome man and sitting next to me. It feels like I have won a lottery.Thought Misha)

"I am Joana's boyfriend, Ron" he smiled back.

"Oh. That girl from Biotechnology Lab" her smile faded.

But she was touched by his humility.They talked and talked.

I am the son of Devaki and Mr Vasudev he said

Misha said "wow! So was Krishna"

Ron smiled in a mystic way

"Are you Indian? I asked as you don't look like one." Curiosity got the better of her as Misha asked the same.

"I am Anglo Indian" he replied

I have psychic powers he said I can help you out

Great really! Show some

He revealed some secrets of Misha's life. "You think you are Radharani but in reality you were Satyabhama in past life, Krishna's wife".

"Maybe I am a devotee of his and I am in love with him."said Misha

"I am Lord Krishna" he playfully said

"Very funny" she nudged him jokingly

"No. I really am Lord Krishna" He then raised his hand and stopped time all around. Everyone there stopped, His handsome face shone with a myriad of aura that lit up the room.

Then the ever compassionate Lord revealed his divine form to Misha. Even the dead stuffed bear rose alive from the dead and touched his lotus feet.

Will you marry me Lord asked as he held a ring in his hand for her.

Misha was stupid she angrily said "You are boyfriend of Joanna. How can I cheat her. I want to become an astronaut, how can I marry" she replied in her dumbness.

"Okay. You are a nice girl, but that's mostly because you are not that mature. You will regret it later" he sadly smiled and said.

He held her poem **In love forever after ..** in his hands and tore it into pieces. "But this is not the end if you believe, lets be friends."

"Okay" silly Misha replied although his handsomeness had overpowered her but still the dream of becoming an astronaut was more important to the childish beloved of the lord.

Then the handsome god talked to her about her life for some time and the time turned normal. He made her forget about what happened. Everyone went about there work again.

Misha thought in her mind Why is this handsome guy Joanna's boyfriend . She didn't want to part from him but made a truce with destiny. Maybe if we meet again sometime.

Joanna looked at Ron from a distance She called him "hey Ron, come here, lets go its getting late"

Oh ok..said Ron looking away from Misha

"Nice meeting you Misha see ya later." He smiled and went away with Joanna.

That handsome boy remained in her heart forever He was her soulmate the one for whom she had crossed seven seas and the dimension of ghosts. But due to her ambition and Joanna she couldn't get her hearts desire. But the story hasn't ended for this is just the beginning. What a looser one may say but I call it destiny.

Misha had become bankrupt. She could no longer talk to her beloved God as she believed the psychics communicated to him.

One day She talked to a famous psychic on whom she spent her last dollars. He told her "you are not Radharani, you need a psychiatrist not a psychic. All these crazy things happening with you are a figment of imagination, Maybe you have schizophrenia,See a doctor". Misha took it seriously and although the ghosts still harassed her she shunned them down as imagination. She didn't have enough money to eat for three days. God's blessing came in disguise of a friend who was a devotee of Jesus Christ. She took her to Sunday brunch in the church,But it was only for Christians. Misha got baptized the next day.

The sumptuous feast was laid on the table. She took some bread, salad and hid it in her bag and ate some cheese cake and juice. She managed food for two days. On the third day a party was hosted at her sorority by the facilitators so god didn't let her go without food. She thanked god for his merciful blessing. Her project was to finish in three days and she had a flight back to India.She borrowed some money from her dad who was not able to send her money earlier due to a bank strike.

She went to the airport. Can I have my ticket please. A handsome man appeared at the counter. Her heart said it is Krishna . She looked lovingly at him, thinking of him to be Krishna. He smiled at gave her tickets "Bon voyage" he said. She went back to her sorority happily.

Her dad called the same day "Misha return the tickets as the flights are married ones, that is there is no time gap between two flights you are to change. There will be very less time between the two flights.So go to the counter and correct it tomorrow."

Okay said she as she hung up. She went to the airport the next day but the counter clerks replied in negative and said it was not possible to give another ticket. She asked for the guy who handed her the tickets but the counter clerk said there was no such man there.

She called the psychic again she still believed they could talk to god. There was another psychic this day. She said "Krishna will help you today,He will come in a blue shirt today".Misha believed it again, naive as she was.

 Her phone rung. It was her dad."Where are you now?" he asked.

"Papa, Today Krishnaji will come to help me don't worry" She said there was so much faith in her words that Lord Krishna was touched and he decided to help her.

She went to the airport again. She saw the man again. She rushed to him. He wore a blue shirt and white pants. It was Lord Krishna. "Hey!" Said he "and aloha you come again to meet me in my dreams princess"quoting a line from her poem.

Misha rejoiced and he happily helped her out he looked up at his computer when the clerk was out.

Gave new flight tickets to Misha. She kissed him on his cheek for his help and touched his feet in respect. Soon he disappeared. "I'll meet you again dear..not yet no more." And that was last thing that Krishna said.

She called her dad and told him what had happened. Finally she boarded the plane and went back home to India. Her parents greeted her at the airport.

"See how slim you have become" said her mother. Her father hugged her overjoyed at seeing her again.

Her life became normal again. She went back to Ludhiana. Also she realized the truth of psychics that they were fooling her for money. She became a devotee of Lord Krishna.

Her zeal for her soulmate had not ended. She decided to ask god for her soulmate. There was a cute little Krishna temple, a Kilometre away from her hostel.

She says that I lie

unaware as she knows not,
that in her dreams i lie,
every moment with every breath,
i love her and yet i lie..
those eyes still sparkle
when she softly smiles
and all i say is that i love her
and all she says is that u lie!
still sometimes i wonder
why do i never wry
though of the world she hath o care
yet secretly to me
she just stands and stares
her eyes as round as a pie
and then she softly smiles
all i say is that i love her
and yet she says that u lie!

She started walking bare foot to the temple to ask god for her wish from Lord Krishna.

In the burning sand in the scorching heat she walked and walked till the temple arrived each day for few weeks. The idol of Krishna just stood there still as a stone. One day the lord decided to test her.

She started walking barefoot like everyday but suddenly the chief warden arrived so to avoid ruckus she took the smaller path to the gate. The smaller path was sandy but she didn't know it was also thorny. She by mistakenly stepped on one inch long thorn stick hidden in the roots of a bush. It hit her hard but she didn't bother. So determined was she that she walked along without bothering about the thorn that stuck. When she entered the temple the idol of Lord Krishna shone bright with divine aura. It was lord who had appeared in his idol. His idol was smiling with divine aura as if his soul had entered it for his dear devotee. True devotion can change the heart of stone even and he was the god.

It was symbolic of the fact that no matter how hard you pray a little faith can make you reach the lord.

Misha was overwhelmed. She thought to herself He is so handsome, I'll be his devotee and I'll do penance to get him as my soulmate. She had come to ask a soulmate from him but she had lost her soul in his divine darshan.

She had a rajasthani friend named Vijayshree didi with whom she had moved in.

She was a cook in her hostel and was having some marital dispute with her husband. That's why she was living separately with her three children. She was very beautiful. Misha and she bonded very well. Vijayshree didi decorated Misha herself in Rajasthani costume for Lord Krishna and clad in a ghaghra choli and odhni. It was Vijashrees dress as its customary for married women in rajasthan to wear Ghaghra choli.She would dress up in new dresses for Lord donning lehanga for him and Rajasthani dresses. She'd sing him hymns and songs all the way to his temple. She had fallen in love. She would make bansuri for him with thread and flowers. Whenever she did something for Kanhaji his idol would shine and smile for her.

Chapter 3

The New Birth

The conditions at Misha 's house had worsened with her mother diagnosed with cancer. Her Mother was in immense pain.

Her mother's failing health took a toll on Misha. She fell ill and had fever. One day her fever increased many folds. The temperature had soared high and Misha couldn't even breathe properly. She felt like she was going to die.She removed all her clothes due to the heat. She thought let me think of lord Krishna last time as I didn't chant all life. Did nothing much in his devotion, let me think of him last time.

In chapter 8, verse 10 of Bhagwad Geeta it is written that

One who, at the time of death, fixes his life air between the eyebrows and in full devotion engages himself in remembering the Supreme Lord, will certainly attain to the Supreme Personality of Godhead.

Thinking thus she chanted the Hare Krishna mahamantra.

Hare Krishna Hare Krishna Krishna Krishna Hare Hare

Hare Rama Hare Rama Rama Rama Hare Hare

Suddenly she felt as if someone was touching her forehead. She opened her eyes and to her surprise Lord Krishna was lying upright in front of her, with his back towards the wall. He was looking very worried with his face stressed out and beautiful eyes focused on Misha. He was wearing a yellow dhoti with tilak on his forehead. He caressed her hair flicks,calmed her burning body and hugged her.

Misha looked with astonishment.Never had such a handsome man ever come to her or for her. He held her hand as if comforting her. It was winter but Misha was not well, she did not even give him a blanket, but it was not her fault. She was dying that day and couldn't do much. Then she thought maybe it is imagination. Or maybe the fever had gone to her head because of which she was imagining things. She kept her leg and knee on his hips.

Krishna was offended. He suddenly pushed her leg with force. Then Misha realized that it was real. Krishna said "go sleep you 'll be fine"and he disappeared after that. Misha slept after that, the fever slowly subsided.In the morning as she opened her eyes, a new life awaited her. The sun looked fresh with life. God had saved her and given her a new life..

She gratefully thanked him and decided to be his devotee all life.

Flower Murli as made by Misha.

Soon holi had arrived. In a white kurta and pyjama she went to the temple with Vijayshree didi to play holi with Kanhaji. As she took a phera, a round of the temple idol, gulal appeared on her cheeks as red dots on her face. Vijayshree laughed at Misha when she saw her face. What! what is there to laugh at..she asked unaware of what happened.

"There is gulal on you face and dots on your cheeks and ear. Who played holi with you?" Vijayshree asked merrily.

What! I didn't play holi with anyone. She replied back where did it come from.

"Maybe Kanhaji played holi with you, Lucky girl" said Vijayshree.

Its not possible.. said Misha with disbelief in her eyes.

She took another round of the idol

A big dot appeared on her nose and Kurta.

Vijayshree was surprised now.. "See on your nose she pointed out."

Misha couldn't believe still she took some gulal and applied on Gopalji's lovely face.

She took a round again and he again put dots on her face and gulal on her hands and this time her kurta was red with dots made of gulal.

Misha got scared. They both prayed to gopalji to not play with them as Misha was scared.

After coming back from the temple she decided to make food for Lord Krishna.

She made prasadam with Rice and curry and placed it on a banana leaf for her sweetheart. The kind lord was very happy. He appeared in front of her for the first time. He was very handsome and dressed in a peetambar yelllow coloured dhoti and with jewels adorning his neck. He ate the prasadam and disappeared.

Misha was very happy. She happily went back to Vijashree's room. She became more sincere towards her work after that. She went back to her hostel room. She would work hard all day long in the clinic thinking that maybe god would be happy. An animal owner even complemented that she was the most hardworking of the doctors. She was working on a burn patient those days who happened to be a calf. She worked all day to treat her patient with care. In the evening she went to the temple to see her Krishna's idol.

It'd smile back to her and shine with aura if she worked hard enough. Soon Valentines day appeared. Misha decided to make a Teddy bear for Lord Krishna.

She took some clay and made a beautiful teddy bear with it. As she placed it in front of Krishna's idol, Lord Krishna's idol shone with bright aura and such romantic feelings emerged out of him Misha melted like a melted ice cream. It was amazing and such love emerged out of Krishna's idol that she forgot herself for one moment.

Misha was overjoyed.

Clay teddy bear as made by Misha.

Next day she found a puppy in front of the clinic. Someone had abandoned the poor fellow. Its rear legs were paralyzed but the little pup was a happy go lucky one. Misha decided to adopt him. She took the little pup to her hostel room. She adopted and took care of him. She named him Cotton Munna.

The hostel girls weren't happy with cotton so they complained to the warden about cotton. So the warden scolded Misha. So she went back to Vijayshree didi's house. Vijayshree didi was poor and lived with little money she got from the mess she worked in. She had a photo of Lord Krishna she prayed to.

Misha made beautiful murli's for Kanhaji each day working hard all day long. She had to prepare for her pre PG exam but it was very tough. Meanwhile She had not given up her dream to be an astronaut. She would work hard at the gym. Run Km's and Km's for her dream.Her degree course and internship had ended.She had to go back to Ludhiana.

Soon her internship came to an end. She decided to go to her grandmother's house.

Lord Jagannathji floundered for her love,it was such a torment to the supreme one. Maybe he thought their love will come to an end if she left. She went to the temple that day but Krishna's idol was very sad. Misha consoled him and said it won't end. She thought that one who is omni present will be present everywhere. How can our affair end. But Krishna was unconsolable and depressed that day. He wanted Misha to stay with him but she got a call from her grandmother. She decided to visit her grandmother instead. When Vijayshree got to know that lord Krishna was upset from Misha she gave his idol some makkhan to eat and prayed to him to console him. Lord Krishna was happy he took the makkhan and the makkhan appeared on his photo as if god had taken the bhog of makkhan. He emptied the bowl of makkhan. He was touched with Vijayshree's kindness and was angry with the selfishness of Misha.

Next day Misha came to Vijayshree didi and she recounted the incident. Misha slapped herself for such stupidity. Lord Krishna didn't appear after that in the temple idol. She went back in tears to Ludhiana. There she got selected for PG in a premier university by grace of Krishna. Lord was very kind to her in this.

She went searching for him in every temple of the city. Her father took her to all the temples of the adjoining area. But none of the idols responded and stood like non living idols on the altar. Misha was loosing faith but she decided to try one last time on a beautiful temple located at a chowk. As she entered the temple the idol of Krishna smiled in front of her. It was a beautiful idol standing there. Adorned with beautiful jewels and peacock feather crown he looked lovely in a velvet dress. His rose-sandalwood fragrance filled the temple room. There was compassion in his eyes. Maybe the lord's heart melted at her determination.

Misha rejoiced at it.Her eyes filled with tears and so did her father's.Her Krishna was back but not that willing to reconcile so easily. "I won't give up dear and I am sorry" said she as she walked out of the temple after taking the prasad.

Lord smiled and blessed her.

But just one smile..

Insane I went in that lotus eyed one

The divine in him the compassionate one

A drop of dew.. a passion divine

A piece of love so subtle and sublime

Romantic sophistication didn't seem to matter

When He smiled at me, in the rains pitter patter

His face that had lines of concern

My beloved my baby, I am your fawn

Whatever I am is for you

From you I shine, from you I dawn

Everything I am is just for you

As your curls fall on your face as you laugh

The world comes to a halt in your passion divine

Just know that you exist

Just that is enough for your beloved

Oh my sweetheart, But just one smile..

Oh my sweetheart, But just one smile..

Lord Krishna responded little now. Six months had passed.

Time went by and she made many murli's/ flute for Krishna and worked hard for her career. She started teaching tutions as a part time teacher. When she would cross the busy bridge she would be very scared. Lord

Krishna sensed it and came over bridge to support her and to waive off her fear. She saw Lord Krishna in his four handed lotus form on the bridge whenever she passed on it.It was a heavy load bridge.

Oh the handsome debonair he was. No one could but be lost in his charm.Those beautiful brown eyes, those beautiful curly hairs that fell on his shoulders and strong arms.The peacock feather crown and his smile that pelt the moment into ice.His dew soft lips that remained pristine. That oh my lord you are so pure that you may not be defiled. The divine aura that surrounded the bridge in his grace. Misha felt blessed and wished to be his wife.

 She started walking bare feet to the temple again.

Soon it was valentines day. Misha was very confused as to what to give to the supreme being. So she decided to surprise him. At 4 am, Misha got up. She collected a leaf with dew drops and collected some more dew from flowers and leaves. She placed them at the lotus feet of Lord's idol. Lord looked at it. He smiled, Misha went back happily. In the dawn as the day begun, it was a holiday that day. Her friend Astha came. She started talking to her. She was a fellow devotee. They would discuss Krishna together. Thinking about his pastimes and beauty and their longings for him. "So how are you didi..what did you gift your krishna on valentines day" she asked her.

"I gifted him a pearl necklace" said Astha

"I gifted him dew drops dear." Said Misha looking sadly. "I hope he likes my humble gift to the one who has it all."

Suddenly Astha stopped and everything came to a halt. Her head went back and god emerged from her. Lord Krishna came out smiling in his four handed lotus form.

His face shone like the sun. His aura filled the plethora of the environment around. So magnificent, so divine. It filled her with ecstacy.

He explained her how all sentiment biengs are part and parcel of his existence and how god is the one acting through all of them. This is his supreme maya and how under the influence of this maya the people think them separate from god and spend their lives searching for god who lives in them and beyond them. She could even see his presence in every being around that day.

When Astha normalized she didn't remember anything. Her memory was washed of the moment as if woken up from a trance.

Her dew drop had worked. Lord gave her a beautiful gift on valentines day, so beautiful that she could never forget. She became filled with ecstasy. She danced and danced for lord Krishna all day dressed up in a beautiful dress for him. Most awesome valentine's day to remember.

Chapter 4

Lord's universal form: A tryst with the supreme

Days passed by. Misha's Mother had passed away with cancer recently. She was treated in the best of hospitals yet the doctor's medicine worked to no avail.

She would sometimes appear as a ghost to her occasionally but Misha got scared so she prayed to god and he made her mother's ghost go away. She was very attached to her daughter and couldn't bear separation from her family. It was a huge setback for her family and her mother.

Death indeed is a transient phase as after death there is a new life.

Misha would dance for lord every day, it would help her forget her pain. Decorating herself with flowers and jewelry. One day she prepared a beautiful dance for lord on the song "Moh Moh ke dhage". She quietly sneaked out to the roof of her house. Dressed in a beautiful peacock dress she danced as if in a trance for the supreme. The whole galaxy was visible in the clear night sky at 3 am in night.

Suddenly Lord appeared from a distance in his supreme divine universal form, known as the viraat swaroop. Divine conch shells played all around. Divine music filled the sky. There were angels dancing in the sky. Galaxies dancing around him and all the planets filled with joy but they didn't know why as lord kept it a secret. She could see numerous forms of lord with uncountable heads,eyes,hands and feet and bodies. All smiling lovingly at tiny little Misha. The supreme excellency in might and power was also supreme in his handsomeness and gentleness. Misha was filled with awe, she rubbed her eyes. It was too much for a human to usurp. God gave her noble eyes to see him in his universal form. Suddenly the ghost of her mother came. She looked at Misha concerned but there was detachment in her eyes. She looked at the viraat swaroop, and the clouds appeared and hid the handsome god's face. Now Misha could see only his body. Misha didn't look at her mother.Her mother smiled and went away. He compassionately came back in his four handed form divine lotus form. Misha bowed down with respect. Lord smiled and gave her a rose for her hair.

Her eyes filled with tears. Suddenly she heard some sound of rattling of the door. "I have to go lord" she said to her lord and rushed to her room below and hid in her blanket. It was her father who'd got up to check the doors. Lord Krishna smiled at the innocent girl. Maybe it was his wish.

She meets him again

"Yes today my lips are sealed
I don't know what to say
all done & said
What you have said
That's all my heart can say
Thine pearl of love
I my heart I bear
Was it a dream
That I had seen
Yes Its true that I love you dear
and yours forever had been
I needn't words
For I love U dear
And you
Know how my heart can beat
So come to me and kiss me dear
Don't beat a hasty retreat
Yes today my lips are sealed
I don't know what to say
all done & said
What you have said
That's all my heart can say.

Now she was of marriageable age. Her father started coaxing her for marriage.

"Now you must get married" said her father

"No" she said "I will marry Krishna only" Misha replied

Misha declined all marriage proposals.

They had an altercation at that and she left home to commit suicide.

Misha was very upset. She took a seat in an adjoining park.

"Pristine in existence, you are supreme

My beloved dear please come to me."

Said Misha to god

She sat there making her last murli for her god with tears rolling down her face.

Suddenly a guy appeared in the park. He looked in his 20's. He came and sat near her.

It was Lord Krishna himself in disguise of a boy. He looked cute and funny dressed in a Multi coloured shirt and short hair. He looked like Raj from movie *Rab ne bana di jodi.*

Sasrikal ji (A greeting among sikhs) he smiled and said

Misha looked up "Sasrikal" she meekly replied

"What are you making dear", he lovingly asked

"I am making a flower murli for Lord Krishna" said Misha wiping off her tears.

"Show me.. You make it daily" he asked

Yes I do..Misha smiled for the first time. She felt a bit uneasy with a stranger.

He took the murli from her hand and sat next to her.

"Hii.. I am Moninder" he said to her "I live nearby"

"I am Misha,I make these murli's for Krishna said she" as she wiped off her tears and shook hands with him

"You make beautiful murli's dear." said Moninder looking into her eyes,such that it made her blush.

"He is a total stranger to me but it seemed as if he is an angel from god." Thought Misha

"Hey I am not an angel.I am god himself" laughed Moninder.

"What! Very funny"..said she as she became cross a bit at that

"No dear I am not joking, I am really Krishna, your love".

Why are you sitting in the park?" he asked

Misha couldn't believe her eyes

This simple rustic boy is claiming to be Krishna, Iam sure he is just a naughty boy teasing me.

Then the great lord held a sudarshan and conch shell in his hand, " see I really am him" saying thus he gave her his divine darshan .

That four handed handsome beauty had no one parallel to him in this world.

She said "oh you are really Krishna." She kissed him on the cheek.

"Will you be my wife". asked Krishna

Misha thought of her hubby Krishna sitting in the idol at her home

Misha smiled and said "my Krishna is at home waiting for me in the idol

I will never leave him"

Krishna smiled "Ok dear, your wish". He caressed her flick and kissed her.

Misha was on cloud nine..that cloudy day,the dusky cold weather

Cool breeze blew her hair more. Kanhaji held her hand and kissed her.

"It seems like you love to wait for me" said Krishna

"I do dear" said Misha then they kissed each other

Suddenly her phone rung

It was her father..he had cooled down.

"Where are you" her father inquired

"Papa I am in the park I am coming" said Misha

Krishna said time to go baby, "tell your father that you are with his future son in law."

Misha smiled "really you are very funny".

"Ok baba I am going now." Bye said Misha

"Ok dear" said Krishna sadly and Misha went back home.

It started raining on her way back home.

The idol of Krishna shone brightly as she loved her idol and caressed it with her arms. Krishna saved her life that day.

Trance of love

For so long I've been so drear, beloved dear
And let us to the tone of ecstacy dance
For this I the sweetest music of all
And the maples gushed in with the wind
The clouds still thundered in the rain
And all could see that we did dance
With our souls entangled with a fretless tone
The melsh of weather, the kiss of rain
A little tryst, his and mine
Mingled with a feeling of love divine
The dark washed streets were not a sore to sight
But the moonlight made the dark to bright
And then with my touch his beats I felt
A moment curbed and a moment felt
To the pitter patter in his arms I pelt
Who knows with this moment
How together we dealt
And how I blushed in his charm and poise
Or maybe it was just a cunning ploy
Oh joie de vivre!
We danced and danced, this jingle of the thunder
No jazz no jejune
But something of the heart, and something of the tune
With soft caress of his fingers, with softness of his smile
He knews that there was pain in my heart

That I hid in a smile
He asked me is there love in your heart?
I asked him do you have a doubt?:)
So it was love that then I felt
And my tears of joy, just he could feel
As all washed with the rain..

So time passed and an amazing opportunity came. The swiss space tourism agency called applications for astronauts. Misha applied in that. She was filled with excitement. Happiness filled her heart more,She felt closer and closer to her beloved Krishna. She emersed herself in training and her PG work. She worked on sero-epidemiology and protein biomarkers of a disease. She completed her research work soon and submitted her thesis. She was now a post graduate.

Swiss space tourism agency called her up. Their space programme had been canceled because of some technicality. So now her space dreams had come to pause but she was a fighter she didn't give up. She got a job in Ambala as a Veterinary surgeon in a government veterinary hospital. Misha's dad thanked god for his mercy. Finally her dreams got a flight. Her bigger dream was to reach lord Jagannathji.

She got posted in a far off village in Ambala. The path was dainty and it got scary at dusk. Yet it was fun working there with no work all day and work came only during their monthly meetings. But it was lonely at home with only Krishna to talk to so she'd immerse herself in her devotion making different things for Krishna all day. She made slippers with craft stuff for baby Krishna. Lord

Krishna himself came and wore the slippers in a child's form. Her slippers increased in size and she touched his lotus feet and helped him wear the slippers she made for him.

It was beautiful life there still. She'd adore Krishna and imagine him when she missed him. She would imagine making love to him at times. Long time had passed with no call from her beloved Krishna.

One day a peppy young gentleman came to her. He was the Veterinary surgeon of another village. He was handsome and stylish. His name was Aditya. They met at a meeting in Ambala. They soon became friends. He was a chatterbox. He would chat with her all day long, texting her whenever free. Misha felt relieved to have found human company at last. She didn't have many friends so Aditya became her best friend. He lived nearby but they only met for work. One day a case arrived.She had some issues with her work. Aditya helped her out and Misha was relieved. Soon vaccinations arrived. They had to vaccinate animals of 15 villages.

Her compounder was a good hearted man but of a harsh tongue. He lacked manners to talk. He was often rude and rest of the staff was also lazy. Misha one day scolded him in front of everyone. Misha was a bit apprehensive of him so she asked her Krishna to scold him for her.

Her compounder Rohit was texting her as to how he was unable to go to door to door to vaccinate animals. Misha said in anger "You are useless, there is nothing you can do properly not even your own work". Rohit felt very hurt at this. He called an urgent meeting of all the subordinates and discussed the spat with them. God knows what they discussed, from next day he became a reformed guy. He helped her vehemently in vaccination and other office work.

Misha would bathe her Krishna idol with cold water in summers and apply powder on him. One day as she was bathing Krishna, A sweet gentle female voice spoke "My dear won't you apply me powder".

Misha looked above..there was no one she looked below and a dark pristine shadow appeared, it was Radha Rani's she wanted to befriend Misha.

Misha rejoiced at that. Now she had a new friend. So she bought a new idol with Radha Krishna combined. She would take care of them,bathe them,feed them. A new relationship began. Misha would often get late to room so Radharani scolded her and asked her not to be late and Misha obeyed.So they remained friends for long.

Here Aditya was romanticizing about Misha. He liked her as a person.

So he proposed her one day.

Misha declined his proposal gracefully.

She made him understand how she loved Lord Krishna and how she wanted to be his only. Lord was testing her in this.

That day the cool wind blew and at night Lord Krishna came to her window. He was sitting on a Red magic carpet. She got up suddenly ruffled her hair and looked up at the window.The handsome lord was smiling at her.She got up and ran towards him, he was sitting on a carpet that could fly. He forwarded his hand towards her to bring her up on the carpet but Misha was scared. She was scared that she'd fall down. He said if you have faith hold my hand and climb up,but Misha was too scared. It was 12 in the midnight. There was a sharp iron rod gate below. The lord smiled and said you need more courage. He got down from the carpet and walked to her room.The carpet disappeared. She hugged him and they talked for some time, Misha's eyes were filled with love and tears.

Lost in his devotion the time stands still
As he caressed her hairs,he longed for a kiss
Those touches of his passion made her sublime
In his suavity and strength
To feel so weak in his arms,
the power of love, the submission divine
The sun shone late the moon stood still
The space was a witness of their love
Hidden in a blanket just you and her
Oh lord my love just don't leave
Just be in this moment and let me please
Give me the right notes to my chords
Like a guitar just play and play
In the myriad of your smile
Let me make you love oh..Exotic divine
Let me be your maid and you my king
And the stars our subjects just you to please
Let us be one, in every particle
Let not the cosmos or stars know
Just you and you in every cell I breathe

Hare Krishna Hare Krishna only you I feel
He smiled and said just one luck
I'll caress you to the zenith
A flower just tuck, Lets dance till dawn
My baby my fawn, let me touch your soft bossom
the stars and the moon in your eyes dissolve
So he played guitar and played her a song
They made each other so happy as the universe absolved
In his love in unconditional mercy
The true Alexander, The king of the verse
Lost in his poetry, lost in his words
Softly as the magic sublimes, the oceans rose and rose to the skies
She kissed his heart and felt his beats
and to this tune they danced a bit,
His curly hairs, with kisses she adorned
His soft dew lips, soft as dough
And prayed for his mercy, just his to be..
My beloved lord, oh king of verses
Make me thy poetry and submerge in your verse
In his eyes I looked and felt like a queen
They became one in soul, every particle of Misha danced
In devotion she submerged and his she became.
Lost all fear, let alone shame
He looked in my eyes and magic begun
A tune so unheard and song so pristine
All I ask you is let me be yours
come to me and be mine too.

Then Lord and Misha made merry. Angels played songs for some time.Then they got sleepy and Misha dozed off. In the morning she looked at him..He smiled and said "What?" Misha looked at her watch and said "baby I hope I am not late for the clinic, you also have to run the universe..get up lazy bum, I'll make you breakfast". He pulled her towards him and caressed her more but Misha pushed him lovingly and got up. She gave him some milk to drink. He drank it flirting with her hands that held the glass.

"Shit its late" he said it was already 7am and the temples had opened so Lord smiled got up got ready and one last thing he said. He snapped his fingers and Misha forgot everything. Kanhaji was gone.

She looked confused around.There was no one. "I must be imagining what a dream"She said to herself, but she could still smell the scent of sandalwood on the blanket and a guitar was lying near the bed. "When did I get the guitar she asked herself" she said but she was happy she found one, someone must have left it here and she kept it in store place and got up ready for office.

Misha would sometimes play guitar for lord Krishna when free for him.

The work load increased as the government changed. Office became a tension slowly. Her family was pressurizing her to get married.It wasn't easy to handle them. She decided that she will commit suicide but not leave her Krishna. She decided to quit her job and gave an exam for PhD. She wasn't prepared but during the exam she saw lord Krishna sitting near her.

"You lord..wow! Are you here to help me" she softly whispered

"Yes dear" he replied as the lord came near.

He dictated her the answers all through the exam. She quietly smiled and gave the exam. Nobody could see him. She didn't know anything, in her busy routine she didn't get time to study so lord kindly helped her so that she wouldn't give up on life. She stood first in her exam. Misha was overjoyed. She hugged her Gopalji and thanked him.

There is a verse in Srimad bhagwad geeta that says

मच्चित्त: सर्वदुर्गाणि मत्प्रसादात्तरिष्यसि |
अथ चेत्त्वमहङ्कारान्न श्रोष्यसि विनङ्क्ष्यसि || 58||

Bhagwad geeta 18.58: If you always remember Me, by My grace you shall overcome all obstacles and difficulties.

"be my devotee and all your troubles will be gone by my grace,"and so it happened. Lord saved her life again. Her new life began.She became immersed in work and studies. A long time had passed and Misha missed her lord. On his birthdays she'd decorate herself for him and bring in bansuri flute cake,and dance for him. She'd buy silver jewelery for him as it was affordable for a student. Lord looked like a decorated knight in those.

She'd love him dearly but she had to manage work as well. So she worked as well as continued her penace for Krishna. She would do cow seva daily and bring food for the animals who were injured in the veterinary clinic of the hospital. She would sometimes hire men to clean sheds of injured dogs. She cared for the sick dogs on the street and tried to be nice to people.Its called punya siddhi. She thought maybe the lord will appear with this and bless her again. It had been a long time and lord didn't come. Maybe her efforts were not in the right direction. She felt depressed sometimes due to loneliness. Her pain maybe the words couldn't describe.

There were some evil souls who were jealous of her. They were some saints and gods who stalked her in schizophrenia and dream. Misha was still unperturbed, She kept on doing punya siddhi for an year. Slowly started taking the medicine for schizophrenia. Her college was affected, she couldn't do her chores in earnest. But lord helped her as a very kind friend. After that the evil souls disappeared. She became aligned towards buddism and started following lord Buddha. She'd meditate and follow his 8 fold path. She became calmer and purer. She would see his serial made on Lord Buddha's life. The last episode was very sad as Buddha dies, Misha cried all night. As the dawn broke, she saw that Buddha's photo smiled and Lord Buddha shone in that with his brilliant aura and magnificence. He was smiling. It was just to tell her that he is still alive, he still exists. Misha found a guru that day. She offered him soup and he readily took it. They became friends. Misha took the eight fold path seriously and started following it.

Chapter 5

Avalokiteshwara form

Meanwhile by grace of Krishna, She started her work again and worked hard this time. Going to far off villages,collecting blood samples and data. Her research took a jump again and her sincerity increased. With her work going well the lord appeared again. There was a picture of god hung in her mess in which Viraat swaroop of god stood with thousands of his hands. Misha made fun of his hands and started dancing her hands around mimicking him and doing mock Egyptian dances. The supreme lord was insulted. Lord decided to teach Misha a lesson.

Next day dew had not evaporated from the leaves. The cold morning sun shone bright. The wind blew as if welcoming the sun and all auspicious things started happening. The desert city had suddenly become a little heaven for the calves and people going off their business.

In the early hours of the morning a handsome 100 handed god Krishna was standing in front of her mess. She named him as avalokiteshwara form of lord. He danced with his 100 hands and he looked amazing like a peacock attracting its beloved mate. Those soft doe eyes with kajal donned. Those dark black hairs that fell in curls. That smile that could sway an enemy with its magic. He touched her hair and caressed her lips with his. She freaked out in the beginning but then she controlled her fear. She hugged him and some girls started laughing at her. The lord couldn't be seen by others. She got wary and kissed Krishna and went back to her room.

She was happy in the inside that finally Lord Krishna had appeared. She fell in love with him over again.

She peeked form her door. Krishna had went by then, leaving behind a peacock feather for her. She picked the feather and decorated it in her hairs.

She continued her penace in form of cow seva in a temple. It was far off but Misha went their daily working hard for lord. She even cleaned placenta of a recently parturated cow that had fallen on the floor. Meanwhile she missed him more and more. Misha became impatient. She wanted to touch him, feel him, love him again. She started making love with him in her imagination. She'd imagine him and they'd make love with each other for hours.

The lustful lover

My lustful lover, oh insane
Diving me into your myriad ways
Those passionate thrust, those lustful hurts
I broke your heart in my lust I know
If you have love you must show
Come to me oh beloved dear
Let our passion bloom like the rose
Let our love surmise like the moon
Like its peaceful lustful shine
Let the passionate sunrise go
commencing in a loving good night
Your soft heartbeats I want to hear
This pain of separation is hard to bear
So let me kiss you oh passionate one
Be my god and earth so near
I love you and that's all I wanna say
Let me come near your hairs and let me sway
Let me kiss your dew soft lips
Give me courage and let me dip
In your elixir, my baby my love
In your devotion,in every life
Let me dive in the oceans of thine depth
so subtle and sublime,your myriad aura

Soon his words were to come true. Misha thought they
were idols but idols have souls. She didn't know that. They

were demigods that hid in idols. And kept an eye on the girlfriend of the supreme. (Be cautious with demigods, they are not just idols. They are live beings. Its best to stay away from demigods as they can harm really bad in jealousy).

Meanwhile her loving real family had turned mean. They started harassing her for marriage again. Coaxing her to meet new guys for marriage. Misha decided to do penace to undo for the same. She would work hard in her penace to avoid marriage. It worked for her for some time. Soon she met a saint who advised her to read Bhagwad geeta. So she read Bhagwad Geeta. It was a whole new world for her. Such monastic discipline was imbibed in that book that she decided to follow it by heart. Soon she understood that one can reach god even by being his devotee in his normal life by expressing his gratitude. By not leaving his karma

यस्त्विन्द्रियाणि मनसा नियम्यारभतेऽर्जुन ।
कर्मेन्द्रियैः कर्मयोगमसक्तः स विशिष्यते ॥

O Arjuna, one who controls the senses with the mind begins to do so.

He who is unattached to the senses of action and to the yoga of action is superior.

Karmayoga refers to all good, correct human acts implemented with concentration, expertise, and skill for paving the path to salvation (Moksha). It requires your services, activities or deeds to be without any attachment to the temporal world. You can reach god even by doing your karma sincerely and by being lords ardent devotee.

Meanwhile Misha made a new model on Aghasur leela. Legend has it a snake demon named Aghasur gobbled up Krishna's friends. Krishna killed him then and gave his soul salvation in his divine form.

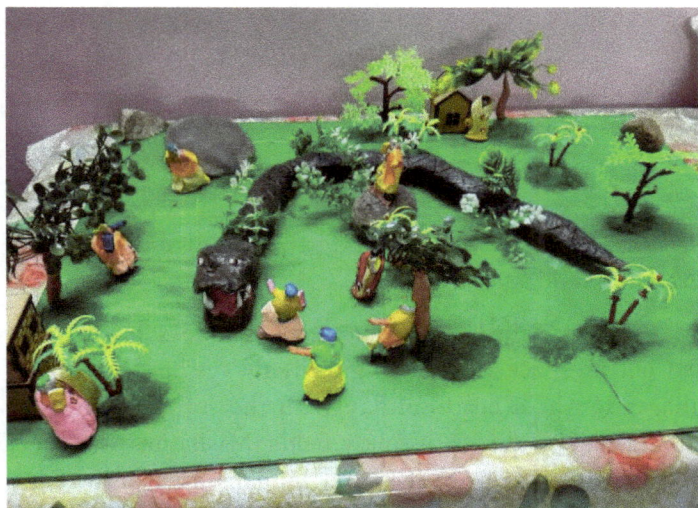

Aghasur in vrindavan village surrounded with cowboys and Krishna's friends. Krishna standing on a rock with Yashodaji near her home.

Chapter 6

The Refuge of Goddess Karni

One day during her scientific trips to far off villages, something very unusual happened. This was a trip to Gadola, a far off village in rajasthan known as a nirvan place for Goddess Karni.

It's a village which was blessed by goddess Karni mata that her presence and blessings will always be there in this village. It was a beautiful day with the soft morning sun shining on the dunes of sandy fields. Misha had to collect blood samples from camels and humans as a part of her research project. She got some medicine for the naive farmers otherwise they wouldn't let her touch the flock or tola.

They spoke in a different dialect of Rajasthan, not understood by city people. The farmer's brother translated his words for her. So they started collecting the samples from camels.

The camel owner lovingly gave them fresh camel milk to drink. It was super tasty with its soft frothy milk and freshness. It seemed heavenly nectar to Misha. The men and veterinary compounders that were with her also drank camel milk.They were the people that restrained the animal and helped Misha collect blood samples. There were 50 camels in total. Most of them were very docile but they came across a camel which was in heat or Rutt season. That means testosterone in him was high and he was in Rutt (Which is a highly excitable state of camel) in this it gets aggressive and dangerous. Camels can sometimes even eat the head of its owner or harm it viciously if disturbed during Rutt.

They needed to collect 50 samples from 50 different camels. Misha was scared of that camel as its mouth was frothing and eyes were scarily angry. If they didn't collect blood from him her sample size would have remained 49.

What happened? asked the camel owner

"This camel is in rutt so we will have to leave it undisturbed otherwise it will attack".replied Misha,looking concerned.

"Don't worry nothing will happen. This is a blessed village. Goddess Karni left her human body here in this village. Pray to Karni Mata and she will help you."comforted the camel owner.Misha prayed in her heart to god to help her and also paid her obeisance to goddess Karni. The compounder started restraining the camel in rutt. Misha was freaking out a little bit and then she saw something amazing. The camel cooled down and Karni mata's beautiful face appeared in the eyes of camel. She was smiling elegantly through the dark black eyes of camel.The anxious camel calmed down as if a lamb.

Misha bowed down and thanked the goddess for her help. It was a beautiful tryst with the divinity of karni. Finally the men took the samples. She became friends with goddess Karniji.They left the village in a happy mood singing bhajans and songs devoted to god.

Chapter 7

The Fruit of Honesty

Misha would do punya siddhi now and then. Krishna's devotion had made her very kind and compassionate. She'd often buy clothes for the poor and feed them. One day she came across some poor labourers. They were children who had no slippers. Misha went to the ATM and as she entered the ATM cabin she observed that someone had left his money stuck in the cash dispenser of ATM machine. Lord Krishna had said that that one should never snatch or steal others right. She did think of donating it to the poor but Misha's heart said " be honest and buy stuff for children from your own money". So Misha took the money from the cash dispenser and submitted it to a nearby bank whose ATM it was.

Beautiful act of honesty. Maybe lord will like my honesty she thought. That day it rained and the weather cooled down. In the sky there appeared a smiliey cloud as a blessing from god. Misha looked at the sky and was surprised. Lord Krishna was testing her in this. Misha brought the children slippers and good clothes just like lord lovingly washed his friend Sudama's feet in love. In the same way Misha touched the feet of the poor labourers and gained their blessings. Her conscience today had something to boast of. That it was honesty she followed.

Cloud smilie as seen by Misha

Months passed without any relief. She was lonely and a bit lost. Krishna had not given her darshan for a long time. She started missing the need of a companion. As days passed by Misha's longing for Krishna increased but her commitment was unwaivering. She tried all sorts of things. She started making flower rangoli's for him. Every day she made a rangoli to please him.

Flower rangoli on valentines day by Misha.

Misha loved making models for Krishna. She prepared a model of Krishna eating makhan.

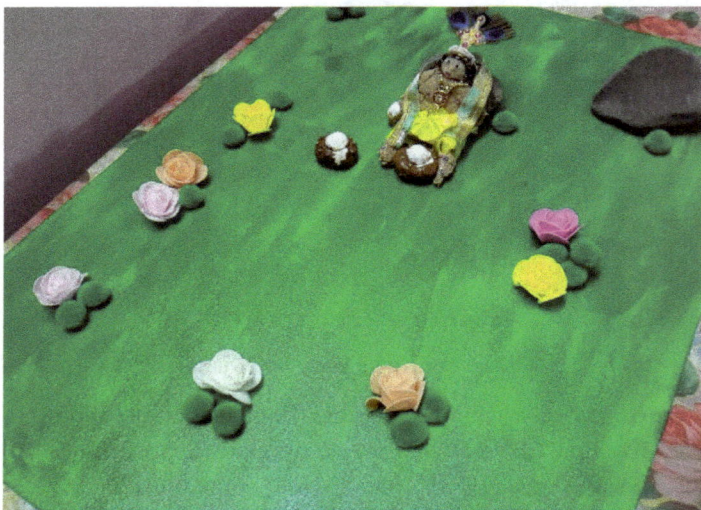

A model of Krishna eating makhan by Misha

Her devotion bore fruit. Lord Krishna was pleased and he gave his darshan to her as Jagannathji. She could see his image in water she offered to Krishna. She could see him everywhere on walls in plants,trees everywhere. The handsome lord not understandable even by the mighty Brahmas is most humble and compassionate to his devotees.

In Bhagwad geeta chapter 7 verse 25 Lord says.

nāhaṁ prakāśhaḥ sarvasya yoga-māyā-samāvṛitaḥ
mūḍho 'yaṁ nābhijānāti loko mām ajam avyayam

"I am not manifest to everyone, being veiled by My divine *Yogmaya* energy. Hence, those without knowledge do not know that I am without birth and changeless."

The devotion of lord's true devotees is stronger than the veil of yogmaya that hides god from us.

Chapter 8

Krishna Meets Again

One day Misha and her family got an invitation from an award ceremony. Misha's father got a call from his ex-student that he had found a groom for Misha. He was a handsome software engineer who was also a Krishna devotee.

When Misha was informed the same she freaked out.

I don't want to marry dad, she commanded but her words were to no avail.

Her dad didn't listen to her and sent her photo and biodata to the boy.

When her dad went to take his award, Misha stole his mobile and texted her dad's ex student

"My daughter is already engaged so we can't proceed further".

No reply came. His ex student felt bad at it and didn't reply after that.

When Misha's father came to know about it he was very angry.

Lord Krishna was touched and he decided to come for his dear Misha.

The function was going on, suddenly a hand rested on Misha's shoulder. It was of Krishna.

"Oh my god its you lord" said Misha as she exclaimed. Her heart bubbled with happiness as she hugged him.

Krishna was draped in a single white cloth. He looked very elite with no jewellery on him. Yet he looked so classy as if that single cloth had been designed by the best of fashion designers.His curly hair and his unearthly eyes did the magic. Misha had never seen him looking so handsome. There was a very pure aura on his face. The best part was no one else could see him. His beauty can be described by one line "husne jana ki tareef mumkin nahi" Its not possible to describe his beauty in earthly words.

Among the crowd of people they looked like two swans intertwined in love. Their eyes did the love making, such pure it had become. They sat in a corner and talked to each other. Misha felt like a maid in front of him as he was so handsome. He held her hands and kissed them. She was so lost in him that she kissed him and that she knew nothing of the world. Krishna got her some tea and they drank some tea together. Lord stopped the time and everybody in the room came to a standstill. She was a bit shy with Krishna as his handsomeness made her feel uneasy as she felt she didn't at all deserve such a handsome guy.

"Misha come here" her dad interrupted. Misha had to leave. Krishna looked sad but happy. He let her go again and disappeared. Misha sadly left her hubby.

Her dad saw Krishna. "Who was the man who had tea with you" He asked her.

"It was Lord Krishna" she said. Her dad didn't believe her but as she showed him the cup it was Krishna written on it, with a peacock feather beneath it.

Misha was overjoyed. She would dress up for krishna in lehanga choli and decorate herself with flowers. She'd walk for miles together to meet her baby... Krishna who'd wait in the temple too. He'd come if it rained. He'd come if shamed but he came nevertheless.She worked sincerely in her institute only to get his smile. His idol would shine for her and talk at times but just for a minute or so. She stood on a stone under the scorching heat. Walked on the sands with cactus bushes.The thorns didn't seem to matter for her. For her love her soulmate was so near. Just some miles away he lived. But to her he was in her heart dear.

Misha would dance for him for hours in a day. One day while she was dancing suddenly a monster appeared to her. He was a demon sent by a jealous demigod who I'll not name due to obvious reasons. It was hideous and scary and looked like a godzilla. He appeared out of the wall over her bed. But her compassion had no bounds. She remained calm nevertheless. In bhagwad geeta its written as below.

अहमात्मा गुडाकेश सर्वभूताशयस्थितः |
अहमादिश्च मध्यं च भूतानामन्त एव च || 20||

O Arjun, I am seated in the heart of all living entities. I am the beginning, middle, and end of all beings.

She was so engrossed in her devotion that she didn't care and kept her faith in god. The monster howled dangerously so much so that lord Shiv was also stunned and surprised. Misha kept dancing and dancing for lord Krishna. Lord appeared for her and caressed her. He said I am here for you not for your dance. He was concerned about her safety but his presence made her feel safe. Seeing the lord the monster disappeared out of fear as Lord held out his sudarshan and scared him.

Truly there is nothing to fear as its Lord Krishna, who plays all the roles of this universe. All the roles that people get in their lives due to their karma is due to their ignorance. The reason people fear is due to their attachment to fear. Which is called "मोह" attachment.

Misha's laddu gopal who she worshipped and loved.

Let me dance and let me sing and decorate for you our lovely nest. Let me huddle and let me care. Whether the sun shines or it rains whether I live or I die I shall still be yours my sweetheart that my heart yearns for you. Keep my faith in you oh my ocean.For my beloved darling your yogini waits for you.For my beloved darling your yogini waits for you.

Chapter 9

The Curtain of Maya

One day she was sitting with her friend Rohit and they were talking about their lives. It was evening time and the weather was cool. The garden was quiet with not much people.

Rohit was very upset about his breakup with his girlfriend Priya. He said you seem close to Lord Krishna. Can you please ask him if my girlfriend will return or not. Misha smiled said "anything for you yar". She closed her eyes and thought of Krishna. She said yes as Krishna said yes in her mind. Suddenly it thundered a bit. She looked above and saw that lord removed the curtain of maya it was like peeling of a fruit. A portion of the sky didn't look like the sky. She could see the lord smiling handsomely like a debonair and his spiritual aura filled the evening sky.

He wore an awesome crown and wonderful jewels. He seemed to control everything like puppets. All men and women strolling about the street and on the grass were like puppets in front of him. He appeared huge, covering a portion of a sky and he had removed the curtain of maya from the sky. All the birds, men and the trees appeared to have Krishna in them. Tears welled into Misha's eyes and Rohit was also bewildered at the same time. He too saw the same. She loved it the amazing way the curtain of maya disappeared. No words can describe the beauty of that wonderful event. One year later Rohit called up Misha. "Hey do you know I met that girl Priya again . She called me up.Your Krishna was right"he said.

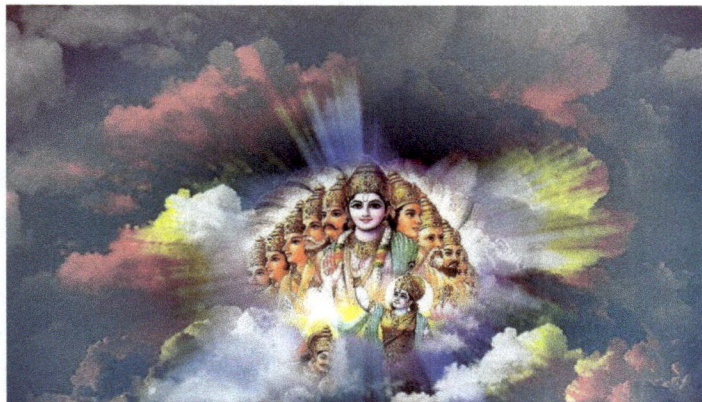

Krishna in his magnificient form as appeared to Misha.

Our Karma is influenced by our ego and if you are a true devotee of Krishna, whenever sin comes to our heart its best to submit ourselves to god and chant the Hare Krishna mahamantra. This mantra saves us from sin as sins have reactions. Every action has an equal and opposite reaction. Why suffer by doing sinful activities. Its best to dance and rejoice in his mercy instead of wasting your time on sense gratification.Please senses of god instead.

Chapter 10

The Marriage Demon

Parents are a rare class of species who do so much for their children whether boy or a girl but when a girl gets older they are anxious to give her to someone else who did nothing for her and yet gets to enjoy her to the fullest. Girls are forced to leave their house in name of marriage. Its tough to fight parents and the same was for Misha. A brave goddess can fight a thousand demon but the demon of marriage is hard to fight. Most often people give in to him.

Her dad had found a rich guy for her earning 2 lakhs a month. Misha was not interested in him. She was broken inside.

"Beta we will not live for long.Its you're duty to get married for your family it's a sacrifice you must make". Her dad brainwashed her for an hour so that she might agree. Misha started crying. She saw her laddu gopal then. He too started crying for her. Both lovers went their hearts out and hugged each other. Then Misha went into the prayer room and started dancing for Krishna.

She danced and danced for him till Radha rani suddenly appeared. She was too touched by her devotion. She too started dancing with her. Then when she began to go. Lord Krishna appeared in the sky. He looked amazingly handsome. His beauty too divine to withhold.He was smiling at Misha. It was a symbol of his presence with her. Misha slept peacefully that day.Just as she was beginning to get used to her destiny, her dad called the boys family.

"Yes Bhaisahab" he said "you didn't call"

"No bhaisahab, we feel the girl is too old for our boy so we won't be able to proceed "saying thus they refused the alliance. Misha was saved.She hugged her laddu gopal and kissed him a hundred times thanking him for saving her.

Misha started meditating then. She'd work in the day in her office with utmost sincerity and at night she'd engross herself in devotion. Her family would not let her do the ekadashi vrat. They felt it was a waste to keep such fast. But then Misha had a solution. Secretly she'd feed the poor on the day of ekadashi. One day she fed 10 poor people living in a slum near the railway station.Lord Krishna appeared to her in a dream and said doing such will remove your sins and you will get more good karma than one can get by fasting. Thus she'd secretly help the poor.She'd also teach poor children. Due to good karma her tamsik guna disappeared and she became more pious. There was a sweet small temple in the city she'd often go to. It was a one roomed temple with very sweet idols of Radha rani and Krishna. Misha would bring flower garlands for them whenever she passed by. Now there was another demon that appeared. The demon of unemployment. Misha was on a contractual job and her famiily often taunted her with that. "Ask your Krishna for a job if he is so capable.These gods are useless" said her folks.Her father believed in Karma only. Misha then studied day and night and cleared her NET exam. It was by Lord's grace that she was able to clear it. She sincerely accepted it that had it not been for his support she couldn't have cleared it. Her family was overjoyed,yet they said it was due to your hard work and not because of Krishna. Thankless people one may say..

Chapter 11

Misha Runs Away to Her Zenith

Meanwhile the marriage demon reappeared again. This time the marriage was finalized. The more Misha resisted the more her parents forced her to marry. She finally agreed and gave in to her parents pressure.The marriage day came. She was dressed as a bride and wished for Krishna as a groom.Krishna knew that her heart was only for him.Tears welled up in her eyes. Her makeup has screwed up a little bit. She started singing bhajans and hymns again.

As her time came near she decided to give it one last try.She removed her bride clothes and dressed up as a maid. Somehow hiding herself from the guests she came to the temple.

She walked bare feet till she reached the temple. On entering the temple she ran straight into the temple and she finally had darshan of Krishna and her happiness knew no bounds. She was stunned and screamed with extreme happiness. She drank the nectar of his beauty. She then ran towards him and touched his face, embraced him and her soul rested on his lotus feet and was totally consumed. Thus Misha who was completely immersed in his love got relief from sansara as she totally desired & happily united with her lord. She closed the temple gates and started dancing in front of his idol.

Misha's father knew exactly where she could be found. He called the cops.

The police found her by her mobile location. They came to the door of the temple and knocked it. The voice of hers singing bhajans could be heard out loud.

"Come out here at once madam the police is here" shouted the police. They kept banging the door but Misha was unperturbed with this, she kept on singing bhajans for Krishna.

The police broke the doors and bang it opened. Misha was filled with tears.

The police tried to catch Misha but Lord Krishna then came on Garuda. The policemen were scared and astonished. The Garuda flapped its strong wings.

The mighty lord was very angry with Misha's folks and the police. The police left Misha.She ran towards Krishna.She smiled into his eyes so pretty. As he looked lush in his charm divine. After all he was the most handsome man in the world. "And yogini we meet today, the melsh of weather you understand, come jump on Garuda fast" saying thus Lord Krishna offered her his hand and she took it jumping on Garuda's back happily and off they flew away to his pious dimension Golok.

Later they got married in Golok dimension. She did come back to her parents but this time with sindoor on her forehead and a baby in her arms. Her old parents were overjoyed. Whatever they did was in ignorance so Misha forgave them because their love was very pure.

They only wanted their daughter to have a settled life.

So her folks also forgave her as they loved her and they fell in love with Krishna too. They were happy to see Krishna as their son in law. Misha's father fell at Lord Krishna's feet and sought to repent for his actions. Lord Krishna said "No father I am your son in law now it is I who should touch your feet to take your blessings." And saying thus he hugged her father.

Misha met her zenith her beloved soulmate

Oh god I love happy endings.

Hare Krishna Hare Krishna Krishna Krishna Hare Hare

Hare Rama Hare Rama Rama Rama Hare Hare..

Zenith

Long I waited in your pursuit
My zenith my love as the fortune teller foreseen
My love you do understand
The melsh of weather
The soft dew rain
With you as my master and me your gopi
Krishna Krishna your name I chant
With stroke of love,my lover sublime
Mingled into my lover's tryst
They flew past the sun into the skies
She smiled and looked into his eyes
As he looked lush in his charm divine
This worldly matters now consign
As their souls mingled into the divine
To this he picked her up in his arms to his lap I undersign
The touch of his lips and his curly hairs
The yearning of his heart to that of mine
My love my baby I give up
And to your charms I now resign
And to your charms I now resign

"And that's how I met your father" said Misha to her little four year old daughter as she kept her novel on a side by the bed.

"Really father, is it true that you escaped on the Garuda.."Asked the little one curiously

 Krishna said and smiled "yes that's how I met your mother".

"Now go to sleep you have to rise up early baby"saying thus he kissed his daughter.

He kissed Misha as she curled him up in her loving arms..

As the angels played lyres for the baby to sleep.

The breeze blew soft as the stars shone in the beautiful grand palace into the Goloka sky..

9 789364 520461